Among the cream of Viennese society gathered at the German Ambassador's ball on 27 January 1889 was a stunning young woman. In full bloom of her youth at 17, with her luscious red lips parted in anticipation of some great adventure, she seemed to glow with an inner excitement. While she drew everyone's attention with her exotic sensuality, she had eyes for only one — Crown Prince Rudolf, the dashing young heir to the mighty Austro-Hungarian Empire.

Three days later, they were found dead — together.

# DOOMED FROM THE START

**CROWN PRINCE RUDOLF WAS BORN INTO WEALTH AND POWER, BUT HIS FAMILY WAS TORN BY DISEASE AND STRIFE, WHILE MARY VETSERA HAD A SPOILT CHILDHOOD DOMINATED BY A SOCIAL-CLIMBING MOTHER: THE SEEDS OF THE MAYERLING TRAGEDY HAD BEEN SOWN EARLY**

*Graphische Sammlung Albertina, Vienna*

👑 *Rudolf Franz Carl Josef above was greeted at his birth with cannon salutes, tears of joy from his father, disbelief from his mother and general jubilation in Vienna. As the new-born Crown Prince was named after the founder of the Habsburg dynasty, many were the hopes and expectations invested in the baby, who, it was hoped, as a future ruler would restore the fortunes of the ailing empire*

👑 *Rudolf was heaped with diverse honours and offices at his birth. Many of these he inherited merely by virtue of his exalted position: among them, Colonel-in-Chief of the 19th Infantry Regiment. To celebrate this, the popular Viennese composer Josef Strauss composed the* March of the Austrian Crown Prince, *opus 59 right*

*Wiener Stadt- und Landesbibliothek*

AS THE HEIR TO THE HABSBURG Empire, Crown Prince Rudolf was the scion of one of the most powerful dynasties Europe has ever known. However, he had inherited emotional and psychological handicaps of enormous magnitude.

On his mother's side, he was the product of the quicksilver Bavarian Wittelsbach temperament – alas, all too prone to nervous disorders from generations of inbreeding. From his father's forbears, he inherited a degenerate strain most conspicuous in the infamous Habsburg jaw. As Rudolf's two grandmothers were sisters, the inherent weaknesses of the two ancient houses were further compounded in the Crown Prince. As if this were not enough of a burden, poor Rudolf, more in need of nurturing than most, received the scantest of parental attention and affection.

His mother, the Empress Elisabeth, was universally regarded as 'the most beautiful woman in the world'. The young Franz Josef – an Emperor at 18 – had fallen madly in love with her, though he had been earmarked for her elder sister. But, after an idyllic start, the great disparity between their temperaments – his, plodding, meticulous and detail-bound; hers, whimsical, restless and obsessed with her looks – proved too great to sustain their marriage beyond the required protocol. Increasingly, the Emperor took to his desk, and the Empress to her horses and ceaseless travel.

Into this unhappy and unstable background, Rudolf was born on 2 August 1858 at Laxenburg Castle on the outskirts of Vienna.

## The birth of a prince

After two unsuccessful attempts to provide an increasingly disillusioned Empire with a male heir, Elisabeth once again went into labour. The omens were not good. The huge, glittering candelabrum in the Throne Room had inexplicably crashed to the ground. No one had dared tell Elisabeth. Worse, she later became delirious and was tortured by dark visions of the downfall of the House of Habsburg. Finally, at 10.45 pm, with one final, painful and determined push, her third child was born. Her immediate reaction was to ask its sex. Was it a boy? She was convinced that she had failed yet again. But Franz Josef, kneeling by her bed, was in tears, thanking her for their son.

While the baby vented his lungs long and loud at his christening the next day, Franz Josef invested him with the prestigious Order of the Golden Fleece. But poor Rudolf's golden hour

did not last long. Royal etiquette, Franz Josef's mother Sophie reminded him, demanded that the baby Prince should be put under the charge of a nursemaid – the Baroness Karoline von Welden, whom Rudolf was to know as 'Wowo'; she was, of course, chosen by Sophie. And even though Elisabeth was, literally, bursting with milk, she was not allowed to nurse her son: a strapping Tyrolese was brought in to fulfil this maternal function.

### An innocent victim

Within a few days, Rudolf and Wowo were relegated to separate quarters far removed from Elisabeth, who, caught up reluctantly in unending court ritual, could scarcely visit him once a day. Meanwhile, Franz Josef was away suffering ignominious defeats in Italy. By the time he returned, Rudolf's upbringing had been well mapped out by Sophie, much to Elisabeth's frustration and despair.

To compound this, Elisabeth's joints became badly swollen. There is no record of what followed. However, it has been widely conjectured that she suspected that she might have caught a venereal disease, as she went incognito to a doctor to ensure that she was told the truth. If her suspicions were confirmed, Franz Josef had given her gonorrhoea. That news would have been as shocking as the fact that he had been unfaithful as, from now on, their marriage was embittered and fraught. That may be why Franz Josef, perhaps just as dismayed, now became enormously attentive to her. But it was too late.

Elisabeth decided her best plan was to recuperate in the sun on the Mediterranean island of Madeira. But she had to pay a price: against her wishes, she had to leave Rudolf and his elder sister, Gisela, behind. Two years later, in 1862, she returned home, fully recovered from her long illness.

♛ *When Rudolf was born, Elisabeth* above *could not believe she had given birth to the much-desired son and heir, and kept repeating, 'It's a girl, it's a girl.' Of her first two children, Sophie* looking down posthumously from her portrait on the wall *was born in 1855 and had died of measles in 1857, Gisela* standing on the cushion *was born in 1856. Sadly, her mother never really took to her, though the little Princess had a fonder parent in Franz Josef. However, Elisabeth felt a particular affinity for Rudolf* lying swaddled in her arms, *who early displayed the extra-sensitive Wittelsbach temperament of her own family*

Historisches Museum der Stadt Wien

♔ *A strong, healthy peasant, Marianka above was Rudolf's wet nurse, as breastfeeding was considered to be in bad taste among the high-born*

♔ *Below* **The family Habsburg:** *standing from left Franz Josef, his brothers Ferdinand Maximilian (with his wife Charlotte), Ludwig Viktor and Karl Ludwig. Seated from left Rudolf on his mother's knee, his sister Gisela looking on, his grandmother Sophie and grandfather Franz Karl*

Rudolf was a highly intelligent child who could be very affectionate and charming, with his soft voice and golden eyes. When he was three years old, he laid the foundation stone of a public building and, when he was four, he accompanied his father on an inspection of a military academy. When the students cheered the Emperor, little Rudolf joined in too, waving his hat. Franz Josef was moved nearly to tears. But Rudolf had also inherited his mother's highly strung temperament and only his beloved Wowo could soothe him out of the tantrums he would throw if he could not get his way.

### The precocious Prince

When he was five, Rudolf became very ill with typhoid fever. But, thanks to the loving and diligent nursing of Wowo and his grandmother Sophie, he recovered; Elisabeth was away. Earlier that year, Rudolf had fallen out of a tree and hit his head badly on a stone. Though he recovered, he suffered from headaches, which he was not unwilling to exploit when he wished to get out of doing something he did not want to do.

As Rudolf reached six, the question of how he should be educated sparked off yet another furious row between mother and grandmother. Sophie was steeped in the traditions of the Viennese court and believed she knew the best way to raise a future emperor; she knew the range and complexities of his duties. As far

as she was concerned, the traditional course was the best way of ensuring that the people got the ruler they deserved. But Elisabeth could not bear such a stuffy approach and wanted Rudolf to have a far more liberal education. With Franz Josef's support she might have won the argument, but he backed his mother.

### A disastrous choice

Rudolf's first tutor was Major General Count Leopold Gondrecourt. Had anyone bothered to study his military background, they would have discovered that he was an extremely inappropriate candidate as a child's tutor. He had a reputation for horsewhipping his men for the slightest misdemeanour and was renowned for his foul language. But he was also extremely conservative – which is presumably why he was selected – and, apparently, very religious. However, his devotion turned out to be a sham. He certainly rose at six, but not always to go devoutly to mass. Instead, he disappeared inside his mistress's bedroom, carrying what people thought was a Bible but which was, in fact, his cigar box.

Gondrecourt's policy for toughening up the Crown Prince involved treating him like a soldier. Rudolf was woken at 6 am to be drilled noisily in the courtyard; even in midwinter with the snow falling, he was forced to wash in icy water; and at night he was likely to be

Ullstein

## THE WITTELSBACH MADNESS

Rudolf often feared he was on the brink of insanity, and with good reason: his mother's family, the Wittelsbachs (the Bavarian Royal Family), had so intermarried with their cousins – including the Habsburgs – that insanity was not at all unusual.

One of the most famous Wittelsbachs was 'Mad' King Ludwig II *below*, Elisabeth's cousin. A great patron of the German composer Richard Wagner, he nearly bankrupted his country by building a great many fabulous castles and palaces, such as Neuschwanstein in Bavaria *right*

woken by Gondrecourt bursting into his room and firing off a pistol to test his reactions.

Not surprisingly, Rudolf fell ill. Though some doctors diagnosed diphtheria, all agreed that Rudolf's nerves were in a sorry state. However, unbalked, Gondrecourt set up yet more exercises in character formation. He took Rudolf to a zoo, trapped him within an enclosure and shouted, 'Look out, here comes a wild boar!' The more the petrified Rudolf screamed, the more Gondrecourt continued to shout.

### Caught between parents

Despite Gondrecourt's highly inappropriate teaching methods, Franz Josef stood by his mother's appointment. Clearly Elisabeth had to

## *'He was physically and spiritually more developed than children of his age but very highly strung'*
### RUDOLF'S FIRST BIOGRAPHER

♔ *Born to command: in the uniform of an Austrian officer, Rudolf right cuts a fine figure of a military man – aged five. By the time he was four, he was already reviewing troops, and it was in the army in the company of other soldiers that he was to spend some some of the happiest years of his brief life*

*Österreichische Nationalbibliothek*

## 'The highest duty of the tutor is to apply every means to secure that his disciple will never waver in his religious beliefs'

LEOPOLD GONDRECOURT

♛ *When Rudolf was six, his upbringing was entrusted to male tutors. But the choice of Count Leopold Gondrecourt left was not a happy one – especially for a child as precocious and nervous as Rudolf. The harsh regime of this dubious martinet took its toll and Rudolf collapsed – physically and emotionally*

stand up for herself or be forced into a minor role. So she gave him an ultimatum. If Gondrecourt was not fired she would leave, and this time there would be no coming back.

She spelled out her position in a letter: 'I cannot stand by and see such things going on. It must either be Gondrecourt or myself... It is my wish that full and unlimited power should be reserved to me in all things concerning the children....' And she concluded by fighting for additional powers, which should automatically have been hers in any case. 'I further desire that everything concerning my own personal affairs ...should be left for me to decide.' In short, she was making a determined bid to take charge of her son's life and her own. Her husband dutifully agreed.

### A proper tutelage

To undo Gondrecourt's sadistic influence, Colonel Josef Latour von Thurnburg was appointed the Crown Prince's guardian in September 1865. He was not only humane and honest, he had the foresight to appreciate Rudolf's special needs and, for the rest of his life, Rudolf, in spite of his wavering and suspicious nature, trusted Latour implicitly.

Latour recognized Rudolf's quick intelligence and inquiring mind, and appointed liberal-minded tutors – much to the annoyance of

## Tragic Destinies

| Emperor Franz Josef (1830–1916) | m. | Elisabeth (1837–1898) | | Ludwig (1831–1891) | m. | Henriette Mendel, Baroness Wallersee |

| Sophie (1855–1857) | Gisela (1856–1932) | Marie Valerie (1868–1924) | (1) Crown Prince Rudolf (1858–1889) | m. | Princess Stephanie of Belgium (1864–1945) | m. (2) | Count Elemer Lónyay | Marie Wallersee, Countess Larisch |

Elisabeth (1883–1963) m. Prince Otto Windischgrätz

| Franz Josef | Ernst Weriand | Rudolf | Stephanie |

| Bernhard Vetsera | m. | Carolina Ullmann | | Theodor Baltazzi | m. | Eliza Sarell |

Albin Vetsera (1825–1887) m. Helen Baltazzi (1847–1925)

| Ladislaus (d. 1881) | Hanna (1868–1901) | Mary (1871–1889) | Franz (1872–1915) |

*Tragic Destinies*

Haus-, Hof- und Staatsarchiv, Vienna

👑 *In Colonel Joseph Latour von Thurnburg* left, *Rudolf found a surrogate parent who combined paternal authority with sensitivity and understanding. Rudolf developed a deep respect and affection for 'my dear old man', as he called him, which lasted beyond their official relationship as master and pupil*

👑 *Further additions to the Imperial Family below: in 1873, when Rudolf was 15, his elder sister Gisela married her cousin Prince Leopold of Bavaria. In the meantime, Franz Josef and Elisabeth had had another daughter, Marie Valerie in foreground with dog, born five years earlier*

Bildarchiv Preussischer Kulturbesitz

the conservative die-hards at Court. Rudolf flourished intellectually under the expert tutelage. He was proficient in the many diverse languages of the Empire and he always maintained an excellent command of German.

However, the roots of Rudolf's volatile and unconfident nature were too deeply embedded for even the enlightened Latour to reach at successfully. When he was nine, feeling aggrieved at a lack of recognition, Rudolf wrote out his first will, hoping to frighten Latour into an indulgent response. But the canny guardian refused to succumb to the moral blackmail and responded only by correcting Rudolf's spelling mistakes and making him rewrite the document correctly. Rudolf's morbid preoccupations with death were beginning to emerge.

## Preparing for manhood

When he was 11, Rudolf had his First Communion in the Hofburg Chapel. It was a splendid flower-decked occasion attended by his parents and grandparents, his older sister Gisela, and Wowo, along with the entire staff of the Palace. Rudolf knelt in the red prie-dieu and repeated his christening vows, and later received many presents.

As he grew to early manhood, Rudolf's education became multi-faceted. Not only was he introduced to the various duties of the realm that awaited him, and given a broad scholastic background, he was also initiated into those aspects of life common to all humanity and which are no prerogative of princes. Thus it was that when he was 13, his tutors in their wisdom took Rudolf on a visit to a fish farm to teach him the facts of life. He took to the subject with gusto, as the rest of his life was to show. As a charming young heir to an Empire, Rudolf was to prove an easy bait for the ladies.

his education. For his zeal in routing dissidents during the Hungarian uprising, Albin's father was offered the rank of a nobleman but, sensing that this would endear him even less to the Hungarians among whom he lived, he refused the honour and asked that instead his son Albin be allowed to attend the Oriental Academy in Vienna, which prepared him for his station in later life.

It was while he was in Constantinople that Albin had met and married Helen Baltazzi. Mary's mother had a colourful heritage. Her father, Theodor, was the son of an Italian banker in Turkey who had married a Greek woman. Her mother, Eliza, had an English father and a Greek mother.

### 'The Levantine woman'

Helen Vetsera was determined to establish herself as a society hostess – and in this she was successful, even if her aristocratic guests were not above sniggering behind her back and being somewhat absent-minded about refusing the hospitality of 'the Levantine woman'. Her brothers supplied her with an excellent chef and wine cellar, and no one could deny her impeccable taste in furnishings. Albin Vetsera seems to have kept out of the way in his various postings overseas, and Helen very rarely, if ever, visited him there. As the Empress Elisabeth was horse-mad, Helen was soon mixing with the Royal set, courtesy of her four

# WHO WAS MARY VETSERA?

Baroness Mary Vetsera was born on 19 March 1871 in Vienna. Her very mixed lineage, which combined German, Slovak, English, Italian and Greek blood, contributed to her strange, sensuous beauty which did not fail to attract all men who met her. Her origins were not as humble as the snobbish Viennese matrons, jealous of her mother's social skills, were wont to attribute to her.

Her father, Albin Vetsera, had been knighted and then elevated to hereditary peerage by the Emperor in gratitude for his diplomatic services in Austrian legations in Constantinople, St Petersburg and Lisbon. He retired early but was recalled and sent to Egypt where he died in 1887.

Albin Vetsera's steady rise had been due to

♛ *Like mother, like daughter. Unlike Rudolf, Mary Vetsera had a varied pedigree, a mixture, perhaps, that led to her bewitching looks and the renowned large, arresting eyes – her most striking feature even as a young child* above left.

*Mary's mother, Helen, came from a predominantly Levantine background, though her mother was English. She married a minor nobleman but set her sights even higher. Aspiring to the closed ranks of the very top of Viennese society, she entertained lavishly and threw herself into the heady whirl of country parties, races and balls – such as the one given by Princess Hohenlohe-Bartenstein in 1880, which she attended as 'the African woman'* left

👑 *Mary's parents, Albin and Helen Vetsera, set up house at 11 Schüttelstrasse* left, *a luxurious Viennese mansion which Helen proceeded to decorate with great taste. It was here that Mary was born in 1871. As a young upper-class girl* right, *she was educated by governesses and tutors. The main male influence in Mary's early life, however, seems not to have been so much her own father, who was often posted to the East, but that of her uncles, the Baltazzi brothers: Alexander, Hector, Aristide and* below *Heinrich, to whom fell the task of accompanying Mary on her macabre final journey. 'Intelligent and rich and all having the same beautiful eyes. No-one knows exactly where these people come from,' wrote Countess Festetics to the Empress Elisabeth. 'With all their money they make me feel uncomfortable. The brothers are devoted to sport, ride splendidly, and push themselves in everywhere. But they are dangerous to us on account of them being so English and having such magnificent horses'*

brothers who were excellent horsemen. Alexander Baltazzi's horse, Kisbér, won the Derby in 1876; Hector was five times champion Austrian jockey; Aristide was a famous horse breeder and a member of the Jockey Club, and Heinrich, an officer with the Hussars, was a keen horseman with his own stables.

### Fashionable upbringing

Albin and Helen set up house in Vienna at 11 Schüttelstrasse, and Mary was born there. She was baptized Marie at the Church of St Nepomuk, but later chose to call herself Mary, according to the fashion of the time for all things English.

Little is known of Mary's childhood except that, of four children, she was her mother's favourite, and that, under her uncles' training, she had acquired expert knowledge of horse-racing by the time she was ten: she was known as the 'Turf Angel' by the frequenters of Freudenau, the Viennese racecourse.

This lack of knowledge about her earliest years is unfortunate, as there may well have been something in her upbringing – in addition to an ambitious mother and an often absent father – that would have influenced her fateful decision years later at the age of 17.

All photos Hermann Swistun

♔ *The Emperor poses for the camera with his two young children: Archduchess Gisela beside him and baby Crown Prince Rudolf on his lap*

Süddeutscher Verlag

Bildarchiv Preussischer Kulturbesitz

♔ *The young warrior with his sister. Rudolf loved dressing up as a soldier and had several tiny uniforms to wear*

♔ *Rudolf aged about 15, wearing Prussian uniform*

Österreichische Nationalbibliothek

♛ *Baby Mary with her brother Ladislaus, who died in a fire when he was 16*

♛ *Mary* right *with her older sister Hanna, three years before her death at Rudolf's hands*

Hermann Swistun

Hermann Swistun

Hermann Swistun

♛ *Mary at about two, already an exotic, dark-eyed beauty*

*Armoiries officielle de l'Empire d'Autriche*

The Imperial Arms of the Austro-Hungarian Empire *above* are represented by the double-headed Eagle Sable. The Eagle holds a sword and sceptre in one of its claws and an orb in the other, and its heads are regally crowned. The arms are supported by two griffins – a mythological combination of a lion (king of beasts) and an eagle (king of birds)

## STATE REGALIA

# AN UNCLAIMED LEGACY

*As the product of an impressive lineage that extended back many centuries within the Imperial Houses of both Austria and Bavaria, Crown Prince Rudolf stood to inherit a legacy both rich and vast.*

*During his lifetime, Austria headed a powerful empire, controlling a large portion of Central Europe. Had Rudolf come to the throne, he would have done everything he could to revive what he saw as a crumbling power. But all hope of this occurring was extinguished when the Prince tragically ended his life that fateful winter morning in 1889*

## CROWN OF RUDOLF II

This magnificent crown *right* was commissioned by Prince Rudolf's distant ancestor, the 16th-century Emperor Rudolf II. A splendid example of the work of Renaissance goldsmiths, it is fashioned from gold, pearls, rubies, diamonds and delicate enamel work, and topped with a huge deep-blue sapphire. The crown became a majestic emblem of the Austrian Empire but, as its rulers were not crowned, it was never actually used

## IMPERIAL SCEPTRE OF AUSTRIA

This dazzling Austrian sceptre *left* was made for the Emperor Matthias in the early 17th century. Intricate festoons of jewel- and enamel-encrusted gold form the head, which sits atop a staff of narwhal horn. Surmounting the sceptre is an exquisite sapphire – a stone that was thought to protect its bearer against disease

Kunsthistorisches Museum, Vienna

Interfoto

⚜ All of the Imperial shields of the kingdoms and provinces of the Austro-Hungarian Empire are illustrated *left*. In the centre is the double-headed eagle that supports, on its breast, the shield of the Monarchy. This shield is divided into sections, with a rampant red lion with a blue crown symbolizing the House of Habsburg, a white and red central panel denoting Austria, and three white ailerons (wings) for Lorraine. Encircling the Imperial Coat of Arms is the Collar of the Golden Fleece

The Order of the Golden Fleece dates back to the 15th century, when it was founded by Philip the Good, Duke of Burgundy, to celebrate his marriage to Isabella of Portugal. The origin of the name of the Order has been disputed since the early days of its inception, though it seems to refer to the Greek myth concerning the fleece of a winged ram stolen by Jason and the Argonauts. The 17th-century example *below* is encrusted with diamonds and large garnets

Claus Hansmann/Schatzkammer der Residenz, Munich

Kunsthistorisches Museum, Vienna

♛ At Rudolf's christening, Franz Josef laid the Order of the Golden Fleece in his cradle. In the portrait *left*, the Crown Prince, aged about 22, wears the Order around his neck. An older, much more elaborate example of the Order is shown *right*. It is smothered in diamonds and features an unusual collection of brilliant triangular and rose-coloured gems. Princes used to swap these precious adornments among themselves, thus passing them from kingdom to kingdom

♛ *Below* This stunning collection of jewels was a wedding gift to Crown Princess Stephanie from the City of Budapest in 1881. Each intricate piece is a sumptuous confection of precious metal, jewels and exquisite enamelling. The Egger Brothers, creators of the jewellery, signed and dated the chain. Although part of the Princess's personal collection, Stephanie gave this set back to the Imperial Family when she married Count Elemer Lónyay in 1900. They now belong to the State of Austria

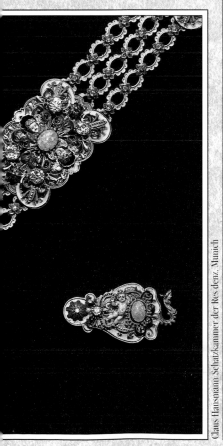

Claus Hansmann Schatzkammer der Residenz, Munich

# AN IDEALISTIC YOUTH

**AS RUDOLF APPROACHED MANHOOD, HIS IDEALISTIC POLITICAL IDEAS PROVIDED A SHARP CONTRAST WITH HIS DISSIPATED LIFE STYLE. SURPRISINGLY, HE WAS ENCHANTED BY THE PLAIN PRINCESS STEPHANIE OF BELGIUM**

♔ *Archduchess Sophie had completely taken over the upbringing of the two elder Imperial children and, when she died, Rudolf was deeply affected. He is depicted below standing next to his sister and behind the Emperor. His mother kneels in front of the body lying in state*

♔ *This portrait of the 17-year-old Rudolf captures the gentleness of the young prince. His tutors, some of the best academic minds of the period, encouraged Rudolf to develop his ideas about politics along the progressive lines then emerging in Europe, much to his father's concern*

**W**HEN THE ARCHDUCHESS SOPHIE DIED in May 1872, the 13-year-old Rudolf was morbidly fascinated by all the details of her passing away. His early adolescence was marked by a developing interest in death and dying. One day, walking in Schönbrunn Park, he heard screams and witnessed a man in the act of killing himself by drinking caustic soda. For days afterwards, he could think and speak of nothing but this macabre spectacle, and he often wondered aloud what it might be like 'on the other side'.

In July 1873, when he was almost 15, Rudolf carried out his first public engagement, unveiling a memorial to former Empress Maria Theresa at Carinthia and composing his own speech for the occasion. He was an intelligent and precocious youth and, encouraged and stimulated by some 50 teachers in a broad range of subjects, he showed himself a remarkable scholar. There was something of a liberal spirit abroad in Austria in the 1870s, and Rudolf was certainly influenced by it, but Latour was at great pains to prevent Franz Josef from finding out just how free-thinking politically his teenage son was becoming.

## Mature for his years

One of his favourite tutors was Hyacinth Ronay, a Hungarian priest, who was hired when Rudolf was 13. He described his pupil as having 'open, gentle, intelligent eyes ... good humour and childish ease ... He is much more mature than his years; he also has humour and wit.' The two got on extremely well right from the very beginning.

Rudolf came of age officially on 24 July 1877 (a month before his 19th birthday), whereupon his studies ceased and he moved into his own quarters in Vienna. From now on, he would be learning about the real world, and to round off his education and prepare himself for his future position he was sent abroad to Britain in 1878. In London, he visited the Bank of England and Billingsgate and Smithfield markets, and throughout the country he saw for himself the conditions under which people worked. What he saw impressed him. 'England has far exceeded my expectations,' he wrote. 'Life here is magnificent and I strive to get to know as much as is possible.' He found time for social activities too. Queen Victoria was greatly taken with Rudolf, and he and the Prince of Wales became firm friends.

One of the tutors who accompanied Rudolf was Professor Karl Menger. Menger stirred up the rebel in Rudolf by arguing that religion was a potentially dangerous weapon since it could be used for a variety of repressive

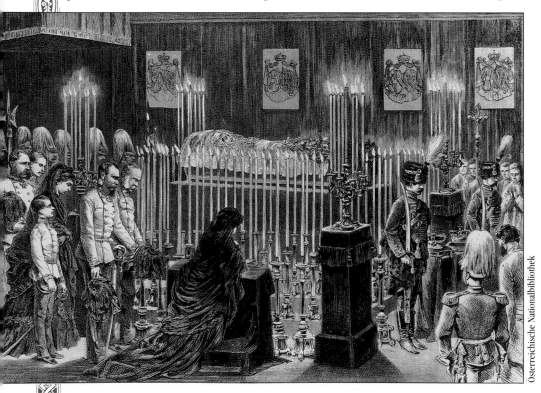

Österreichische Nationalbibliothek

👑 *Rudolf needed the discreet assistance of his servants in his desperate search for love, and he relied to a great extent upon the services of his devoted private coachman Josef Bratfisch right. At night, Rudolf would slip out of the Hofburg by a back entrance and Bratfisch would drive him to a secret rendezvous. But, although there was no shortage of beautiful women eager to become the mistress of the Crown Prince, true love eluded Rudolf until the very end, when he realized he could only find his heart's desire in death*

Österreichische Nationalbibliothek

👑 *The Emperor Franz Josef enrolled his son in the 36th Regiment of Infantry below in the hope that army life would counteract some of the liberal intellectualism Rudolf had learned. Surprisingly, Rudolf loved the army and this interest, plus his excellence as an officer, made a fragile bond between father and son*

political purposes. In this way he prompted Rudolf, already inclined to such views, to reject the Catholic Church, resulting in just the first of many serious disagreements with the Emperor.

## Widening horizons

Another of Rudolf's beliefs to emerge at this time was his mistrust of capitalism. While Rudolf recognized it conferred a great deal on the successful, he also saw that it condemned workers in old-fashioned industries to dire poverty. Rudolf's conviction that 'we should ideally consider more or less equal wealth and prosperity a source of moral development' would have appalled the Viennese Court.

Rudolf's trip concluded with visits to Paris and Berlin. Once again it is clear that Rudolf was no figurehead content to be seen at the right places at the right time. His meetings with the German Kaiser were not simply social events to foster good relations. Rudolf had already decided that a better Europe meant a defeated Germany and had discussed plans with the Prince of Wales for encircling that country when he came to power.

Ominously, while visiting the Kaiser in Berlin, Rudolf shot a white stag during a hunt in the Potsdam game reserve. This – supposedly a portent of violent death – was another of the uncanny omens that punctuated Rudolf's life.

By this time Franz Josef was very worried about his son. Giving Rudolf the finest academics as teachers might have been a good idea in theory, but it had clearly backfired. Rudolf not only needed to be isolated from the world of ideas, but he also needed a career that would turn him into a man of the people and a true member of Court. The solution, the Emperor decided, was the army.

Österreichische Nationalbibliothek

**TRAVEL BROADENS THE MIND**

From the Naughty 90's to the Rockin' 50's...

ICTORY HARVES

**1890 TO 1960**

# 60

## NOSTALGIA POSTCARDS

### — yours for only

# 50ᵖ

Pin-ups, sporting personalities, suffragettes, High Society, The War Years, 'Our Gracie', The Crazy Gang and much more...

**A FASCINATING FREE GIFT TO TREASURE — IF YOU REPLY WITHIN 14 DAYS!**

**YES**

**PLUS! NO OBLIGATION TO BUY ANYTHING ELSE**

...pressed, ...e Order of ...her son's

...Rudolf set ...visiting ...ook called ...is shown ...at the ...of the rich ...to the Holy ...and

...Rudolf ...h he ...I —

...arm heart and ...r beyond his

...delighted. His ...'s future ruler ...t, Franz Josef ...Rudolf to the

...matically en- ...ust as he had ...had to endure

⚜ *Moritz Szeps* left *was the Jewish editor of one of the most widely read Liberal newspapers. He wanted to reform the monarchy, not destroy it, but Franz Josef considered all journalists to be troublemakers whose profession was beneath contempt. Rudolf maintained a friendship with him for several years and wrote many anonymous articles for the free-thinking newspaper*

...of their conservatism. But if he was irked it did not show. He was an excellent leader and cared for his comrades. He knew most of them personally, took an interest in their private lives, and backed them up strongly if they had justifiable grievances. Such respect ensured he was popular with them. One fellow officer described him

*Topham*

unpleasant conditions, so too he spoke out on behalf of persecuted minorities. Jews in Austria had never been popular. Attacks against them went unreported or led to only minimal police action to find the culprits. And there was no pressure from on high for a different approach since most of the aristocracy were anti-Semitic. So, when there was yet one more cover-up after some noblemen had smashed windows and caused a disturbance in the Jewish quarter of Prague, Rudolf defied convention and spoke out. In a much-publicized newspaper article, he highlighted court hypocrisy and made many powerful enemies: 'When a poor country lad smashes a window, there is a great outcry, but when an aristocratic ruffian does so, he is not even prosecuted. The incident is simply hushed up.' The article was not just a defence of the Jews but a clear signal to Austrian aristocrats that when he became Emperor they would no longer be considered a law unto themselves.

In October 1880, Rudolf met Moritz Szeps, editor of the Viennese newspaper *Neues Wiener Tagblatt*, who was to exert a great influence on his life: scarcely a week was to go by in which they did not meet or at least write to each other. Szeps was an intellectual and a liberal, as well as a Jew, and Rudolf's faith in him caused yet more concern to the conservative Austrian Court.

## The road to dissipation

At an early age, Rudolf had been initiated into sexual adventures – it was quite common for an older man to be entrusted with the task of introducing a boy to adulthood via a respectable, discreetly run brothel. The Prince quickly developed an appetite for sex; he was determined to catch up on the love he had missed out on at home – from wherever he could find it.

One of his tutors, noticing a change in Rudolf, wrote to him with fatherly advice that he would have done well to heed: 'You need not empty the cup of life greedily like one who had thirsted for a long time. Enjoy life at a moderate pace...'

Not all his liaisons were fleeting. When he was about 20, he fell hopelessly in love with Maria Antonia, the daughter of the Grand Duke and Duchess of Saxony. They met each other often, and corresponded. Rudolf very much wanted to marry her, but his father opposed the match vigorously. Not only was Maria not grand enough, she was too ill to be counted on to produce an heir. And in this respect he was right – she was soon to die of tuberculosis.

It did not take Rudolf long to take up where he had left off – girls and women queued up for the dashing young Prince and he did not say no. There were so many that Rudolf kept a 'register of conquests', in which he separately listed

♛ *Rudolf's personal life was public property. Princess Aglaja Auersperg above was a friend of his younger sister Marie Valerie, but gossips linked his name with hers. Maria Antonia of Tuscany right was his first love. The pair continued to meet in spite of the Emperor's disapproval, but Maria was already ill with the tuberculosis that would soon kill her. His last lover was noted for her sultry Oriental looks, but the woman reputed to be his first mistress could not have been more different: actress Johanna Buska's vivacious and aristocratic blonde beauty far right was the talk of Vienna when she arrived in that city in 1874*

## A FATAL LOVE

While visiting the Jewish quarter in Prague, Rudolf chanced to see a cantor singing a body to its grave. Near the cantor stood his daughter, a girl of great beauty. No words were necessary. Her father took her away to the country to try to cure her infatuation, but she ran away back to Prague and stood night after night in the moonlit winds of winter, gazing up at the Prince's window in Hradz Castle. By the time Rudolf learned of her vigil, she had died of pneumonia. Rudolf never forgot the cantor's beautiful daughter and made secret visits to the Jewish cemetery *right*, bringing roses to lay on her grave

Bildarchiv Preussischer Kulturbesitz

♛ *Rudolf's letters show clearly that he was genuinely in love with Princess Stephanie of Belgium below, but her own writings reveal a cold and self-centred attitude towards their relationship. There was nothing Rudolf wanted more than a happy marriage. If Stephanie had been interested in him rather than his title, perhaps the course of history might have been changed*

those who had climbed into his bed as virgins. But irrespective of the experience they brought, all left with the same gift – a traditional lover's present of a silver cigarette box.

Yet there was something highly disturbing about Rudolf's relentless turnover of women, whether they were aristocrats or prostitutes. What was he after? The ultimate sexual experience, or a partner whom he could love and trust? He nearly found the latter in Mizzi Caspar. She arrived in Vienna in 1879 and became his mistress for the next nine years.

Given Rudolf's insatiable lust for women, it is no surprise that his parents were delighted when he had completed his formal education and could be sent abroad. They were praying he would find a wife, which is what he did.

### 'Happy and satisfied'

In March 1880, on a visit to Brussels at the invitation of King Leopold II of Belgium, Rudolf met the King's daughter, Princess Stephanie, and somewhat improbably she stole his heart – despite being immature even for her 15 years, very self-satisfied, yet lacking in the intellectual curiosity that was his hallmark. She was tall, plump and awkward, with small, close-set eyes; a good complexion was her only asset.

'I have found what I sought,' he wrote. 'Stephanie is pretty, good, clever, very well bred, and will become a faithful daughter and subject of her Emperor and a good Austrian. I am very happy and satisfied.' They were betrothed within 24 hours of their first meeting. 'I am intoxicated with happiness and contentment. The days pass all too quickly,' he said.

But Rudolf's excitement was not shared by his mother. As far as Elisabeth was concerned, Stephanie made a poor match for her son; she didn't like her, and she was only a Coburg – small beer in comparison to the much grander Habsburgs. But Franz Josef was content.

Bildarchiv Preussischer Kulturbesitz

# THE HOFBURG PALACE

*Stronghold of the Habsburgs since the late 13th century, the Hofburg stands in the centre of Vienna, a rambling collection of royal residences and offices grouped around courtyards. Not much stands of the medieval parts, but among the magnificent baroque buildings, dating from the early 18th century, are the Leopold building, the Church of St Augustin, which houses the Vienna Boys Choir, and the Winter Riding School*

Marianne Haller

E.Graner

The Hofburg dominated 18th-century Viennese social and political life. *Left* A view from St Michael's Place, with St Michael's Church on the left and the old Burg Theatre in the middle foreground

The Emperor arrives at the Schweizertor (the Swiss gate) *below far left*. It was built in 1552 and leads to the Schweizerhof, one of the few remaining medieval buildings of the Hofburg

Even the horses dance under chandeliers in the Hofburg. The white Lippizaner stallions of the Spanish Riding School parade in the Winter Riding School *below*. Descended from original stock brought from Spain to Lippiza in present-day Yugoslavia, they are a legacy of the days when the Habsburg dynasty spanned Spain and Central Europe. *Right* Rudolf performs the Capriole – though he is more likely to have achieved it in the artist's imagination than in reality, as he was never more than an average rider

Archiv für kunst und Geschichte, Berlin

Bundesmobiliensammlung, Vienna

♛ The Amalia wing houses the apartments of the Empress Elisabeth. The functional furniture of her dressing-room *right* makes it almost austere. The austerity is softened, however, by the innate luxury of the room's more permanent features, such as the ubiquitous chandelier and ceramic stove and the gilding on the ceiling and wall panels. An intimate atmosphere is created over her dressing table with pictures of horses and dogs – the chief passions of her life

♛ Many of the beautiful rooms of former state apartments are preserved in their original form on view to the visiting public. *Below* One such room, with a portrait of the young Franz Josef flanked by scenes of military victories, serves as a reminder of the former power of the Austro-Hungarian Empire

♛ The appropriately named Red Drawing Room or Boucher Room *above* forms part of the Imperial Apartments of Franz Josef in the Imperial Chancery wing. The Rococo interior and furnishings, highlighted by the 17th and 18th-century tapestries based on paintings by Boucher, reflect the tastes of past Habsburg emperors

♛ The sprawling Hofburg is often referred to as a city within a city. Interconnecting the various wings and apartments are 54 staircases, such as the one *right*, with its marble balustrade punctuated by gilt urns. Essential arteries of the Palace, many of the staircases have names, such as the Confectioners' Staircase or the Eagles' Staircase

All pictures: Marianne Haller

# THE CRUMBLING ICON

### MARRIAGE TO PRINCESS STEPHANIE AND THE BIRTH OF A DAUGHTER LET RUDOLF SNATCH A FEW BRIEF YEARS OF HAPPINESS – THEN EVERYTHING STARTED TO GO HORRIBLY WRONG

S TRANGELY, IN THE RUN-UP TO HIS wedding day Rudolf became extremely depressed. This may have been no more than the usual bout of nerves and self-doubt but, judging from the description by Countess Marie Festetics, Elisabeth's lady-in-waiting, Rudolf might have sensed he was about to make a terrible mistake. 'As I stepped out of my room... I suddenly felt ice cold... I heard the dear, sympathetic voice of the Crown Prince: "Countess Marie, don't run away, wait a little." I did, and I felt apprehensive for he looked so serious, no, so nervous and so despondent... "For God's sake, say something cheerful to me." Tears ran down my face and I said, "God bless

> ## 'He looked so serious, so nervous and so despondent'
>
> COUNTESS FESTETICS ON RUDOLF BEFORE HIS WEDDING

you and may you be very happy..." This was the prelude to the wedding.'

Despite this ominous attack of nerves, Rudolf pulled himself together for the wedding. Held at the Church of St Augustin on 10 May 1881, it was one of the great events of the day, watched by Europe's leading dignitaries, monarchs and churchmen.

Stephanie wore silver brocade; her train was trimmed with garlands of roses – an outfit considered unsuitable for a girl of 17. With her parents on either side, she marched down the aisle to the waiting Rudolf with 'all the daintiness of a dragoon', according to Archduke Wilhelm.

One of the best descriptions of the wedding comes from Stephanie's diary. After the marital vows and the exchange of rings, 'the church windows were shaken by the reverberation of artillery salvoes; the church bells throughout the town began to peal; they announced far and wide throughout the capital that the wedding had taken place! Shouts of acclamation rose from the populace. The regimental bands played the national anthems of Austria and Belgium. I had been made Crown Princess of Austria-Hungary.'

### A feeling of foreboding

After the ceremony, the wedding guests were treated to a stand-up buffet lunch which, apparently, lasted all of 20 minutes. Then, Stephanie continued, 'I made my farewells. All eyes were filled with tears. I found it hard to tear myself away from my parents. But now the Crown Prince had appeared. He informed us that the parting could no longer be deferred. It

👑 *As Crown Prince Rudolf and his Belgian bride were married in Vienna's Church of St Augustin, the rest of the city had already begun to celebrate the event in the streets. Grand electrical displays illuminating the date of the wedding below, and a magnificent firework show that evening, were all part of the festivities*

Bildarchiv Preussischer Kulturbesitz

*Bundesmobiliensammlung, Vienna*

was time to leave. He led me away... I was alone with a man whom I hardly knew! I was siezed with sense of overpowering dismay as twilight slowly fell.'

## An uncomfortable honeymoon

It was now Stephanie's turn to sense that something was very wrong. And in the short term she was right. The honeymoon was marred by two things: their accommodation in Laxenburg Castle was chilly, sparse and unwelcoming, which helped to make Stephanie's sexual initiation a frightening event. As she angrily wrote in her diary: 'What a night! What torments, what horror! I had not the ghost of a notion what lay before me, but had been led to the altar as an ignorant child! My illusions, my youthful dreams, were shattered, I thought I should die of my disillusionment. I was cold as ice, my teeth were chattering, and I shivered with

♛ **The Allegory of the Engagement** (above) *glorifies the union of the Crown Prince and Stephanie. Rudolf symbolically offers the city of Vienna, silhouetted in the background, to his bride-to-be*

♛ *A second painting commemorating the engagement right brings the two families together. This was probably the young couple's most blissful period – Stephanie looked forward to becoming the Crown Princess of Austria-Hungary and Rudolf felt he had found a loving and supportive wife. However, the Empress Elisabeth was unimpressed by her son's choice and perhaps foresaw the difficulties Rudolf would encounter with this spiritless girl*

*Interfoto*

*Historisches Museum der Stadt Wien*

*☙ An informal portrait showing the Emperor and Empress meeting the Crown Prince and his wife right. In the distance is Laxenberg Castle, where both couples spent their honeymoons*

*☙ Rudolf and his bride are pictured shortly after their wedding below. The early days of their life together were happy ones, as Rudolf was anxious to make the marriage a success. However, he was unable to give up the patterns established as a bachelor, and kept up his military and political involvements. Stephanie, a stranger in a new country, was denied the company she so needed and soon grew bitter*

*Archiv für Kunst und Geschichte, Berlin*

terror. To crown everything, the weather was horrible, rain and snow beat against the window panes.'

Back at home, however, life picked up. The couple were very much in love and were extremely well received at countless receptions. In fact, the social strain became so great, with thousands clamouring to see the new bride, that Stephanie had to be ordered to rest.

But the high life could not continue forever, and gradually Rudolf slipped back into his army career. Stephanie wrote: 'The Crown Prince was much occupied with his military duties. He spent most of the days with the officers in the barracks... After that he would go out shooting... I scarcely saw him.' The first cracks to split the marriage began to appear, though Rudolf was still content.

### A little Archduchess

In 1881 Stephanie's loneliness was temporarily abated when she thought she had become pregnant. But if her private emptiness was not to be filled with a child, at least her public life was crammed full of State occasions in which she learned her role as future Empress. Two years later, though, she really did become pregnant. Rudolf was overjoyed, and planned what they were going to name the baby who, he was sure, would be a boy.

Stephanie's mother came over from Belgium to be at the birth, which was long and difficult. To Stephanie's dismay, she gave birth to a daughter, denying Rudolf an heir. But Rudolf was far too unconventional to be bothered by that, and was delighted with their beautiful child, claiming, 'Little girls are nice and affectionate,' and boasting, 'She is very lively, screams madly, and drinks a lot without any fuss.' The child was baptized Elisabeth, which was shortened to Erzsi.

At this time Rudolf was a great favourite

## HIS FAITHFUL MISTRESS

**Mizzi Caspar came to Vienna from Graz in 1879 when she was 15. She was introduced to Rudolf by Frau Wolff, a notorious *madame*, and soon became his mistress. This was to prove the most enduring of Rudolf's relationships.**

**Mizzi was uncomplicated, amusing, unambitious – just the woman Rudolf was looking for. He fell in love with her, and she with him. But his love was not strong enough to make him want to live, and he told her he was contemplating suicide as early as 1883. At first she didn't take him seriously, but when, in the summer of 1888, he asked her to join him in a suicide pact at a war memorial she went to the police. Unfortunately, she was more or less ignored.**

**In his will, Rudolf left Mizzi enough money to buy a house, and a letter that was 'overflowing with love'**

Hermann Swistun

with the public. One of his most exciting speeches was at the opening of the Electrical Exhibition in 1883. He cleverly and inspiringly used the image of light as a metaphor for his new world, radiating with progress, bringing honour 'to the Empire and to our capital and residential town of Vienna'. The public could not have been more excited. But Rudolf's many enemies read into this new world a tearing up of the old order. The Prime Minister, Eduard Taaffe, and all the leading aristocrats of Vienna were conspicuous by their absence – they were wary of the future Emperor. The secret police kept a daily record of everything he did and said. Rudolf was a marked man.

### The end of happiness

The tranquil domestic life of Rudolf, Stephanie and little Erzsi was not destined to last long, and gradually Rudolf became immersed in his own life. He worked extremely hard at being a soldier, and life with Stephanie was becoming difficult because she just was not cut out to be a general's wife. She wanted domestic security and lavish comfort, when moving from one military base to another provided just the opposite. So she nagged constantly, and the divide between the two increased.

And the gap became even wider as Rudolf took advantage of the scores of women at Court only too keen to oblige him. His night-life was one of the great talking points of the day, and then there were the stories of his illegitimate children: no-one knew the real count but conservative estimates suggested half a

*'He is rather pale, gets about too much . . . He ought to stay at home with you more than he does'*

FRANZ JOSEF TO STEPHANIE

*This picture of little Erzsi dressed in the local costume of Ischl right was taken in 1887. Erzsi was Rudolf and Stephanie's only child. Rudolf had hoped for a male heir, but he loved his daughter greatly and referred to her as the 'only thing that remains of me' in his farewell letter. She, in turn, upheld his memory after his death and even followed in his political footsteps*

dozen. But there was a much more serious aspect to Rudolf's casual liaisons.

Rudolf had caught gonorrhoea when he was 17. In addition to infecting scores of women, he repeatedly re-infected himself. As the disease took hold, so his nerves went and his reactions slowed down. These were particularly hazardous symptoms for a hunter. When he was in his mid-20s, he had a frightening experience. He had fired four bullets at an approaching bear, bringing it down. But suddenly it reared up and came straight for him.

An uninfected Rudolf would have had few problems. But, riddled with a disease that affected his nerves, he failed to grab his cartridges and was only saved by the exceptional bravery and loyalty of an attendant who threw himself in front of the enraged animal. His gun jammed inside the bear's mouth and fired off a bullet, killing it instantly.

### A dread disease

Friends knew something was badly wrong. Rudolf looked shocking – he had aged years in a matter of months, and was plagued by raw, puffy eyes. If anyone should have recognized the symptoms, it was his parents. But either they were too immersed in their own lives to notice, or they didn't want to face up to a son who was betraying all their expectations. His illness

Österreichische Nationalbibliothek

♛ *As heir apparent, Rudolf was becoming increasingly concerned with what he saw as the stagnation of the Empire. His speech for the opening of the Electrical Exhibition in 1883 below reflected this concern and his progressive outlook. But while his remarks were enthusiastically received by Vienna's middle class, a subtle but powerful opposition to Rudolf's opinions was expressed by the absence at the exhibition of the aristocracy and, more importantly, the Prime Minister himself, Count Eduard Taaffe right, who was the Emperor's right-hand man and confidant*

made Rudolf turn to drink and smoking, which only complicated his condition. Eventually the Court had no option other than to acknowledge officially that Rudolf was ill. Of course they did not reveal the truth. Instead, they cleverly let it be known that he had peritonitis and a bladder infection: they named the symptoms but not the cause.

To hasten recovery and keep away from the public gaze, Rudolf went to the Yugoslavian island of Lacroma in 1886 – and Stephanie went with him; by now she had caught the disease from him. Gradually, both pulled through, though Stephanie had become sterile.

Sometime in the 1880s Rudolf also became infected with syphilis – a disease which could cause blindness and heart disease, and destroy the brain. At the time, it was incurable. Rudolf didn't stand a chance.

Franz Josef was so worried by the idea that Rudolf and Stephanie's condition would remain on record that he had their medical papers destroyed. But that should have been the least of his worries. Rudolf was daily looking increasingly unlike a future emperor. His nerves were gone and he was addicted to the morphine he had been taking for a throat infection.

## Saving face

Despite these immense problems, Rudolf did not give up. He tried hard to make up by working hard – but again and again he was found out, or he got onto the wrong end of sharp political manoeuvring. He wrote a perceptive analysis entitled *Austrian Policy*, but it was so out of line with official policy that it was rewritten after his death. In the meantime, he was largely ignored in political circles, adding frustration and depression to his extremely nervous state.

Then, on 3 January 1885, Rudolf was involved in another hunting incident. The Crown Prince and his father were on a shoot and, by

♛ *Although idyllic depictions of the Imperial Family were regularly commissioned, such as this Christmas engraving of 1888 right, the actual image of the family was one of chaos. Relations between its members were strained, and Rudolf's physical and mental health was rapidly deteriorating. He was drinking far too much, addicted to morphine and experiencing dangerous bouts of depression*

the end of the day, had bagged a good stock of game. But as the party was beginning to break up, Rudolf spotted another herd of deer which had come within firing range. His first shot scattered the herd. Too excited to realize what he was doing, he dashed forward, close to the Emperor, and fired again. This would have been an extremely stupid action, even for a first-time hunter. For an experienced shot it was madness. An attendant dashed forward and threw out his arm to prevent Rudolf from accidentally killing the Emperor — and ended up with a bullet shattering his arm.

Franz Joseph was so alarmed by his son's dangerously unpredictable action that he refused to speak to him. When he wanted to find out what Rudolf was up to he relied on the secret police to inform him. But despite his best efforts to keep Rudolf well away from the centre of political and military decision-making, Elisabeth did, for a while at least, haul her son in from the political wilderness; she had at last realized the state Rudolf was in and desperately hoped that if the Emperor could create a special post for him he might be saved.

So Franz Joseph promoted Rudolf to Inspector General of the Infantry, and in the short term this ploy worked. Rudolf was very pleased about the appointment and hoped it would allow him to revitalize the armed forces, particularly as the simmering European political situation suggested that war was never far from the surface.

### The last straw

Rudolf said he would 'vow and hope to be able to carry out my vow in my new position to act in the right way ...' The spirit was willing but the body could not keep up; Rudolf's eyesight was failing and, at a military parade, he was nearly found out: despite being given the tamest horse, the moment it stepped out of line, he could barely cope.

Rudolf realized that his position wasn't taken seriously by the Emperor, and in reality he had barely any influence. According to Stephanie, he flew into the most violent tempers over the smallest issue. 'His inward disorganization led to terrible attacks of wrath, to intolerable and undignified scenes. It was as if, with the loss of inward stability, he had also lost any sense of good form. On such occasions he would not hesitate to talk to me openly about his distasteful *amours*. At length matters came to such a pass that he threatened to finish things off by shooting me and then himself. I was seized with horror.'

Rudolf's adolescent interest in suicide had returned. In late-19th-century Vienna, there was a wave of suicides among the depressed, and accounts appeared in the newspapers reg-

ularly. Rudolf read them avidly, and showed a particular interest in suicide pacts. This morbid obsession should have meant that any woman would approach him with care. Alas, there was one girl who leapt out at him without giving such matters the slightest thought. And, sadly, there was no-one on the sidelines to come to either person's rescue.

*Stephanie* below *did not fulfil Rudolf's expectations. He felt she should have developed with his guidance, sharing his dreams and ambitions. Instead, she continued to feel inferior and became aggressive. Rudolf, who could not cope with the strain, turned his attention elsewhere*

# THE ERA OF THE BUSTLE

*Rudolf's Belgian wife Stephanie lacked the charm of the Viennese and could not compete with the glamour of his lovely teenage mistress. But to achieve the characteristic shape of the time, both women had to endure the tightest of lacing and wear a bustle – a steel cage strapped around the waist to support the voluminous drapery at the back. It was a look that was essentially designed for romance and elegance, rather than comfort*

♛ Worn for her formal presentation to the Austrian court, Stephanie's dress is a riot of frills, flounces and drapery. She wears a corsage of lily of the valley with matching headdress

Corsage of lily of the valley to match flowers worn in the hair

Broad, plain waistband to set off draped bodice

Elaborately draped skirt with deep lace trim

Gloves, fan and lace handkerchief to complete evening dress

Süddeutscher Verlag

Lynne Robinson

This fashionable walking dress *right* is cut from two fabrics, patterned and plain, with the plain forming the underskirt. The small waist produced by tight lacing is emphasized by running the bodice down to a long point at the front and draping the skirt

*'Rembrandt' hat with high draped crown and ruched ribbon bows*

*Skirt draped horizontally over bustle*

*Above* Stephanie in 1908 wears a sophisticated evening-gown and diamonds. The *décolletage* is embroidered with sequins and her brooch complements the elaborate choker. Her hair is dressed high, with a tiara, and she wears a fur stole

*Underskirt of plain fabric to contrast with patterned overskirt*

Ulstein

♛ Mary wore this shepherdess-style dress with its ruffles and pannier-style draped skirt for a studio portrait. The deep bib front is trimmed with bands of fabric in contrasting colours, tucked to match the calf-length underskirt. The overskirt is trimmed with a gathered frill, rosettes and bows

*Choker tied in a bow with cross pendant*

*Bib front with ruched bands*

*Draped overskirt in striped sateen*

♛ Rudolf took great care with his appearance and dressed with impeccable elegance. In this photograph he resembles a romantic poet in his spotted cravat and silk braided jacket, set off by the starched collar and cuffs. A flower buttonhole provides the final touch

Hulton Picture Company

Mary strikes a flamenco pose with her fan outspread behind her head. The full sleeves of her striped dress are three-quarter length, with lace cuffs. Her collar is also trimmed with lace and the front of the bodice has inset panels of plain fabric. The exaggerated shape of the mid-1880's bustle can be clearly seen

The dress which Mary wore to Mayerling, and in which she was burried, was of olive-green cloth trimmed with black silk braid. With it she wore a 'highwayman's' hat' with a turned-up brim and black pumps with high heels. She also carried a muff

Hermann Swistun

*Ostrich feather trim*

*Closely fitting bodice with high military collar*

*Black silk braid*

*Chenille muff*

*Draped skirt over bustle of braided wire*

# A FATEFUL CONNECTION

**THE BARONESS MARY VETSERA WAS BEAUTIFUL – AND DETERMINED.
SHE SET HER SIGHTS ON RUDOLF AND WOULD DO ANYTHING TO
GET HIM. AND TO KEEP HIM, SHE WOULD AGREE TO DIE**

*Turf-Engerl.*

**A**S THE CURVE OF RUDOLF'S FORTUNES nosedived, he had one final affair – his most spectacular.

He was 29 when he met the impressionable, romantic and seductive teenage aristocrat Mary Vetsera.

Their meeting was no accident. Mary had set her sights on the Crown Prince, just as her mother Helen had done years before. Helen was a successful and attractive high-society hostess who organized parties for Vienna's leading artists and politicians. When she was 32, eleven years older than Rudolf, she had attempted to have an affair with him, hastily reorganizing her life to maximize her opportunities for being near him. She flirted so blatantly that the Emperor denounced 'that woman's antics' as outrageous. But where Helen Vetsera's determined campaign did not succeed, her daughter's did.

### 'Pretty but fast'

By the time Mary was 17, she had already acquired a string of lovers; at 15 she had been the mistress of an Englishman in Cairo. But she was not just advanced for her age when it came to men. With her wide, sparkling eyes, she looked more sophisticated than the average teenager. Even Stephanie conceded that she was 'bewilderingly lovely, tall, slender, beautifully made, with small hands and feet; she has masses of dark silky hair and the complexion of a lily'.

♛ *Like many members of her class who were determined to mix with the First Society, the young Mary Vetsera far right was often seen at the racecourse. In fact, her regular appearance there earned her the title of 'Turf Angel' and a caricature in a sports newspaper above left. It was during one of Mary's frequent visits to the races that Rudolf's gaze was first directed to her*

♛ *At the end of the 19th century, Vienna was a gay and lively city that always appeared to be en fête with magnificent balls left and spirited celebrations. But while all classes shared in this passion for life, Viennese society was a divided one. Nowhere was this more apparent than within the aristocracy, which was strictly separated into the smug, old order of the First Society and the ambitious Second Society led by financiers and industrialists*

In conclusion, she was, according to some-one else, 'pretty but very fast'. She was also ambitious: she thought she 'could do better' than the Portuguese Duke Miguel de Braganza, who wanted to marry her. In fact, she had her eyes on no-one less than the Crown Prince who she had first seen at the races at Freudenau when the Prince of Wales was there with him. Edward was a true connoisseur of both horseflesh and beautiful women and could not fail to notice Mary. He drew Rudolf's attention to the dark, sultry beauty. Rudolf made a gal-lant, appreciative gesture of acknowledgement as she curtsied, and Mary was smitten – deeply and, as it would prove, fatally.

### An unbearable life

But while Mary saw Rudolf as the pinnacle of her romantic dreams, Rudolf saw Mary in a wholly different light. This had little to do with Mary herself.

Rudolf's life was becoming unbearable. He was gradually losing his eyesight, was racked with earache and appalling pains in his loins and joints. And his medication, far from curing him, was turning him into a morphine addict.

*'Bewilderingly lovely, tall, slender, beautifully made, with small hands and feet; she has masses of dark silky hair and the complexion of a lily'*

STEPHANIE ON MARY

When Stephanie returned from a trip to Greece she was astonished by the sight of her husband: 'His decay was so greatly advanced as to have become conspicuous. He was frightfully changed; his skin was flaccid, his eyes were restless, his expression was completely changed. It seemed as if his lineaments had lost the inner substantiality... I was profoundly sorry for him, and wondered how the devasta-tion would end.'

She tried telling the Emperor how ill his son was, and begged him to send Rudolf on a long journey, away from everything and every-one who was causing him anguish, but Franz Josef's reply was 'You are giving way to fancies, my dear ... Don't be anxious.' Stephanie later

Mary Vetsera 1886

Hermann Swistun

wrote in her diary, 'I feared the worst – a wasting away which would be more horrible than death.'

An anonymous newspaper article shrewdly summed up Rudolf's position. It referred to signs of emotional unbalance for two years which should have led to his being given professional help, and to hereditary problems – in particular, a marked restlessness on his mother's side.

### The affair begins

For a man so ill, for whom nothing was going right, the sudden appearance of a lively, sensual girl who was clearly interested in him must have come as a tremendous boost.

Their first meeting occurred on 5 November 1888. Mary was brought to Rudolf's private rooms by his cousin Marie Larisch, a friend of the Vetseras. She stayed for an hour. Soon after, she dashed off a letter proclaiming her excitement: 'The greatest wish of my life has been consummated. I have made his acquaintance – I have met HIM.'

And she was so excited that she did not fail to flaunt their growing relationship in front of everyone. In one incident the Viennese aris-

♛ *Mary's father, the Baron Albin Vetsera, was a diplomat who lived in Cairo without the company of his family or the Baroness, who preferred to remain in Vienna. In the autumn of 1887, 16-year-old Mary accompanied her mother and various other members of the family to Egypt see her father, who was, by that time, seriously ill. This picture of the group above, taken next to one of the pyramids at Giza, includes Mary standing at* top, *her mother* right *and her sister Hanna* left *(each marked with a cross)*

♛ *Rudolf also visited Egypt during his trip to the Orient in 1881. He furnished the plush 'Turkish Room' in the Hofburg* right *with items brought back from the tour. The 'Turkish Room' was where Marie Larisch deposited and waited for Mary on the evenings when she had a rendezvous with the Crown Prince. It was also in this room that Rudolf's friend, Herr von Szögyény-Marich, found the Prince's documents on instructions from his farewell letter*

Topham

tocracy watched as the 'other woman' and the wife of the Crown Prince 'fought a duel' with their opera glasses from their respective boxes on either side of the stage. Mary had ensured that she was going to be at her most glamorous that night, and she made it clear that she regarded Stephanie as distinctly second rate. But the real loser of this particular incident was Rudolf. He was in no state to intervene between the two women, nor could he handle a scene with Stephanie.

> ## '*The greatest wish of my life has been consummated. I have made his acquaintance – I have met HIM*'
>
> MARY

Hermann Swistun

## THE GO-BETWEEN

The Countess Marie Larisch was the Empress's niece, of the same age as Rudolf. She was a favourite of Elisabeth and, in 1876 at the age of 18, came to live with her. She was attractive and talented, but unpopular. This may have been partly because her mother was a German-Jewish actress, but also because, according to Countess Festetics, she was 'not sincere – not herself, as if she were acting the whole time'.

When she married Count Heinrich George Larisch-Moennich, Elisabeth gave her a magnificent wedding and an elaborate trousseau, but she was soon bored with her husband and with always being short of money. Perhaps it was this that led her to become a go-between for the doomed lovers.

It was she who formally introduced Mary to Rudolf – for a fee. As she brought Mary into Rudolf's apartment in the Hofburg, a black raven flew at their heads. Had Mary but known what this augured, she might have taken fright – but she was ignorant of the tradition that a black raven appeared whenever a Habsburg was soon to die

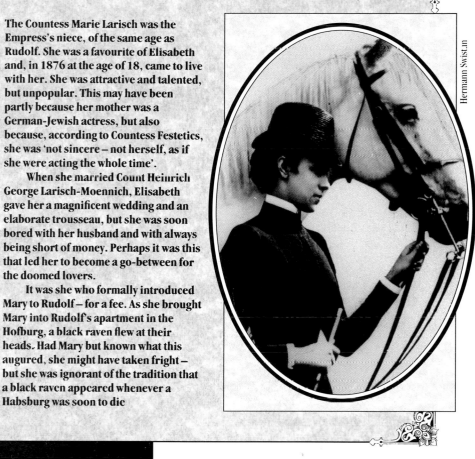

Hermann Swistun

for *In Liebe vereint bis in den Tod* (by love united unto death). She wore it on a chain round her neck.

But they did not become lovers until 13 January 1889. On 14 January, Mary wrote her former governess a note: 'I must make a confession... I was with him yesterday evening, from seven to nine. We both lost our heads. Now we belong to each other, body and soul.' After writing this, she went to an expensive shop and ordered a present for Rudolf – a gold cigarette case inscribed with the date, 13 January, and the words 'Thanks to a lucky chance'.

### No hope for Rudolf

But while Mary was at the peak of her excitement, Rudolf was in despair. He knew the venereal disease he was suffering from was incurable. He knew that insanity ran in the family and he feared he was on the brink. He knew there was no possibility of a divorce from Stephanie. He knew he was drinking too much, but it was a habit he couldn't break. And he knew that, despite his high station in life, he was politically impotent – that no matter how many ideas he had about saving the Empire he considered doomed, there was nothing he could actually *do*.

Mary and Rudolf had many trysts after their first meeting – often arranged and facilitated by Marie Larisch. Once Mary sneaked out of her house wearing a fur coat over her night-dress while Bratfisch, Rudolf's trusted coachman, waited to deliver her to one of the Hofburg's side entrances. And in mid-November, Rudolf presented Mary with an iron wedding ring inscribed with the letters ILVBIDT, which stood

👑 Above *A view of the flat-roofed Augustinergang section of the Hofburg. The roof formed a terrace with a railing extending as far as the Schweizerhof wing where Rudolf's apartments were situated. On the morning of 28 January 1889, Mary and Countess Larisch were escorted over this roof and into the apartments*

## WINE, WOMEN AND SONG

The Vienna of the late 1880s was, on the surface, a bustling, carefree city. One of its biggest celebrities was Johann Strauss. His waltzes – of which the 'Blue Danube' was one – were so popular among the élite of Vienna's society, capturing just the right mood of frivolity, that he was known as the 'Waltz King'. In 1888 he composed the 'Emperor Waltz' in honour of the 40th anniversary of Franz Josef's reign.

Others – today household names – were still struggling to find a foothold. The composer Gustav Mahler *top right* couldn't find an orchestra willing to play his First Symphony. Then, when it was finally performed in 1894, it was panned – his expressive, emotionally charged music was too far ahead of its time.

Gustav Klimt was still an obscure young artist, but soon he would be famous for his highly erotic, decorative portraits of women set against jewelled backgrounds *far right*.

Sigmund Freud *right* was also having a bad time. He had tried curing depressive patients with cocaine, and some had become addicted. As a result, few patients came to see him. But later he was to produce his theories of psychoanalysis and human sexuality that would challenge established ideas of human behaviour

Both ovals Archiv für Kunst und Geschichte, Berlin

Claus Hansmann/Museum für Angewandte Kunst, Vienna

He was suffering to such a degree mentally and physically that, by January 1889, he had definitely decided to commit suicide. But he could not be sure that he could manage it successfully. So he approached a number of people, asking them to join him in a death pact, believing they would give him the strength to accomplish this deadly final action.

His first hoped-for partner was his friend Victor von Fritsche, who promptly turned him down. Next on the list was a fellow officer who also wanted nothing to do with the macabre plan. Mizzi Caspar, his mistress, was next. She alone tried to alert someone, but on explaining his plans to the chief of police was told, as Stephanie had been by the Emperor, not to worry. And when she pressed the matter, she was ordered to forget all about it.

### His last resort

The person to whom Rudolf next turned was Mary Vetsera. Of course, she didn't know she was last on the list. Convinced Rudolf wanted to die out of love for her, Mary agreed – after all, she knew that he would never marry her and, rather than be regarded by the world as an 'ex-mistress of the Crown Prince', she would become a romantic heroine in the eyes of the world and go down in history.

This must have happened very shortly after they became lovers because on 19 January Mary made her will. On 25 January, Mary visited a fortune-teller, and was told she would die in the near future. In the next few days she was to have several attacks of hysteria.

Meanwhile, both sets of parents had heard of the affair and were trying to end it. Helen confronted Mary, particularly over the steel cigarette case decorated with Rudolf's initials and coronet she had received – a gift proclaiming her as Rudolf's mistress. Mary lied her way out of trouble, claiming Marie Larisch had given her the case because she knew how greatly Mary admired the Crown Prince. And when Rudolf was confronted by Franz Josef and ordered not to see her again he assented, provided he and Mary could have one final meeting. But that was all it would take.

♔ *Crown Prince Rudolf as he looked in the year before his death right. Only 30, his hair was already thinning and his outlook on life, by this time, was very dark. Rudolf had talked with a number of friends of killing himself, hoping to form a suicide pact with someone. His mistress, Mizzi Caspar, was the only person to take his threats seriously. She went to the police, but they appeared unconcerned and Rudolf continued his search for a partner in death. By mid-January 1889, he had found that person in Mary Vetsera. She was to become an innocent victim: thinking that the Prince wanted to die out of love for her, she blindly agreed to follow her lover into the unknown*

Bildarchiv Preussischer Kulturbesitz

♛ The richly carved and veneered rococo cradle, made of mahogany and maple and lined with silk *below*, was a gift from the people of Vienna to mark the occasion of the Crown Prince's birth

## TREASURED MEMORIES

# BLIGHTED HOPES

*The longed-for heir to the powerful Austro-Hungarian Empire had a short and unhappy life which came to an abrupt and tragic end at Mayerling hunting lodge in the heart of the Vienna Woods on a bleak January night in 1889. 'The heaviest blow which could have hit a father's heart, the immeasurable loss of my only dear son, has filled with the deepest mourning myself, my house and my faithful peoples,' Franz Josef said. Rudolf's warring parents had battled long and hard over his upbringing, but the death of their only son brought the Royal couple briefly together, united in their terrible grief, as they shared their memories of the bright, affectionate and talented boy on whom their hopes had been fixed*

♛ Rudolf showed talent as an artist from an early age. This drawing *above* in coloured pencil is one of several he made at about eight years old, depicting himself out shooting with his tutor, who accompanied him everywhere

👑 *Left* One of a series of miniatures of the growing Prince. Rudolf was about two when his mother fled to Madeira; photographs and paintings were her only contact with the sensitive, affectionate little boy

👑 *Right* This portrait of their beloved son was painted the year after his awful death. 'Forgive me, Franz,' Elisabeth had said. 'I had no right to marry. Madness is in my family. I have brought it to yours.' But without the verdict of suicide while mentally unbalanced, Rudolf would not have been entitled to Christian burial

Hermann Swistun

# AN UNSOLVED MYSTERY

**ON 30 JANUARY 1889 THE WORLD LEARNED OF THE DRAMATIC DOUBLE DEATHS OF THE AUSTRIAN CROWN PRINCE AND THE TEENAGED BARONESS. WHAT WAS NOT REVEALED, HOWEVER, WAS THE COVER-UP THAT HAS LASTED A HUNDRED YEARS**

♛ *Mary Vetsera above was photographed in a fur coat and plumed 'highwayman's hat', the same clothes which she wore for her drive to Mayerling with Rudolf*

♛ Below *Mary's home. The handsome Vetsera town house was on Salesianergasse in an exclusive part of town. It was pulled down in 1916 to make way for a road*

O N SUNDAY 27 JANUARY 1889 RUDOLF was busy burning private letters and making arrangements with Mary for their rendezvous the next day. That evening he and Stephanie attended a ball in honour of the German Emperor Wilhelm II's birthday. Mary and her mother were also there. Other guests noticed that Rudolf seemed depressed, and couldn't keep his eyes off Mary, who wore a pale blue ballgown appliquéd with yellow and seemed to be 'aglow with some inner excitement'.

Rudolf and Stephanie arrived home by 11.30 pm, and shortly afterwards Moritz Szeps visited the Crown Prince. Szeps later wrote that Rudolf 'was indescribably upset, again and again he repeated: "The Emperor has openly affronted and degraded me. From now on all ties between us are broken... I am free."'

Afterwards Rudolf drove round to Mizzi Caspar's flat where he drank champagne laced with cognac. He told her he intended to shoot himself at Mayerling, a Royal hunting lodge on the outskirts of Vienna. She didn't believe him, as he'd said things like that before. But as he left, at 3.00 am, he – an unbeliever – made the sign of the cross on her forehead. *That* made her wonder.

### The fatal rendezvous

The next day, Monday, Rudolf dealt with routine matters – and possibly wrote some farewell letters – before saying goodbye to Stephanie and little Erzsi. He told them he would be back by 5.00 pm the next day, in good time to attend a family dinner given by the Emperor. Then he drove to the *Roter Stadel*, a restaurant in the Vienna Woods. Waiting for him there was Mary. She had left the Vetsera mansion earlier with Marie Larisch, telling Mary's mother they were going shopping. But,

*Palais Salm Salesianergasse*      *A. Blamauer 1915*

Hermann Swistun

instead, they drove to the Hofburg where Rudolf's valet Nehammer was waiting for them. Fifteen minutes later, exactly on schedule, the cabby Bratfisch arrived in the fiacre to drive Mary to her fateful rendezvous.

Rudolf and Mary spent the night alone at Mayerling, with only a few servants to attend them. The next day, Rudolf's old friend, Count Josef Hoyos, and his brother-in-law, Prince Philip of Coburg, arrived at Mayerling for a shooting party. They were greeted by Rudolf in his dressing-gown, with a silk scarf draped around his neck. In a cheerful mood, he ate breakfast with them, but excused himself from hunting by pleading a bad cold. In a telegram sent to the Hofburg he used the same pretext to excuse himself from the family dinner.

After the hunt, Coburg departed to spend the night in Vienna, leaving Hoyos with Rudolf. They chatted comfortably and dined heartily on soup, *pâté de foie gras*, roast beef, venison and dessert, washed down with red wine.

Mary stayed in Rudolf's bedroom until 9.00 pm, when Hoyos retired to his room in another part of the estate. Then she and Rudolf drank champagne while Bratfisch sang and whistled to entertain them.

In the early hours, the two lovers retired, hand in hand, to the bedroom. The Crown Prince's last words to his valet, Johann Loschek,

## *'Today he finally confessed to me openly that I could never become his . . . So everything is over'*

MARY'S FINAL LETTER TO HER SISTER

♕ **Right** *One of the last photos taken of Rudolf alive. He was very fond of this coat, which he described in a letter as a 'very fine lancer's fur coat . . . very sharp!' He wore it on the final drive to Mayerling*

Interfoto

♕ *Bratfisch drives the couple on their last journey below. In fact, there are no photographs of Rudolf and Mary together. Their heads were inserted into this picture after their deaths, in response to the public interest in the tragic pair*

were 'You must not let anyone into my room, even if it is the Emperor.' And that was the last time Rudolf and Mary were seen alive together.

At about 6.15 am on 30 January 1889, Rudolf woke Loschek. He asked Loschek to call him for breakfast at 7.30, and to make sure Bratfisch was ready with his horses. He then walked back to his room, whistling.

Ullstein

## MAYERLING

Mayerling was a hunting lodge in the Vienna Woods, about 2½ hours' carriage drive from the Hofburg Palace.

Rudolf bought the lodge in 1886, had some conversions done to the building, and purchased a villa nearby so he would have room to put up extra guests during the shooting parties.

The main lodge had a large drawing-room, a dining room, billiard room, bedrooms for guests and servants, plus family apartments. Rudolf's was on the ground floor, and contained a staircase leading up to Stephanie's apartments and a common bedroom on the first floor. Little Erzsi had her own apartments in the former gamekeeper's lodge – these were known as the 'Elisabeth wing'. There was also a kitchen wing and a church. All these buildings, which were whitewashed and roofed with grey wooden shingles, enclosed an internal courtyard.

Rudolf came to Mayerling often, and usually on his own. 'I must have a nook to myself,' he told a friend

Jean-Loup Charmet

♛ *The tale of Rudolf and Mary has continued to fascinate writers and artists up to the present day, but the true story of the events of that bleak winter night have been further confused by such pictures as this 1906 artist's impression of the death chamber* centre. *The tragedy of a young girl's violent death at the hands of her unhappy lover, the implications of Crown Prince Rudolf's suicide and the horror of his last hours are entirely lost in so romanticized a representation of the end of the road to Mayerling*

At 7.30 Loschek knocked on Rudolf's door. No-one answered. He shouted. Still no reply. He tried first the main door, then another door to the room; both were locked from the inside. By this time Hoyos appeared; they both banged on the doors. Coburg now arrived from Vienna, and the two ordered Loschek to break a door down. At this stage Loschek told the two noblemen that Mary was in there with Rudolf, a fact of which they had been unaware. Coburg and Hoyos decided to take the responsibility for Loschek breaking down a door.

Inside they saw the Crown Prince, 'slumped over the edge of the bed with a great pool of blood in front of him'. Lying on another bed was Mary, her body already cold.

### Post mortem

Count Hoyos immediately drove to Baden in order to catch the express train to Vienna – the Emperor and Empress had to be told the terrible news. When he arrived at the Hofburg, Hoyos spent half an hour trying to find someone brave enough to tell Franz Josef. It was decided that only the Empress could do it – but she had to be told first. Baron Ferenc Nopcsa, the Controller of the Empress's Household, was deputed to break the news to her. She burst into tears, then quickly calmed herself when she heard Franz Josef approaching, saying, 'Let him in, and may God help me now.'

Meanwhile, Helen Vetsera had been worrying about her daughter's absence. She sent Marie Larisch to the Police Commissioner twice; both times she was turned away. Growing increasingly desperate, Helen approached Prime Minister Taaffe and was told, 'The matter is too delicate to handle.'

So when, by Wednesday morning, Mary had still not appeared, Helen went to the Palace. Bluntly, Elisabeth told her that her daughter was dead, and then Helen was promptly dismissed with the order, 'Remember, Rudolf died of heart failure.' At this stage, everyone believed that Mary had poisoned Rudolf, but no-one wanted a scandal.

Roger-Viollet

Archiv für Kunst und Geschichte, Berlin

not found, as it made its way out through a bullet hole discovered above the left ear. There can be no doubt that His Imperial and Royal Highness fired the shot himself and that death was instantaneous.'

### Fond farewells

And to support the suicide theory were the various letters found in Rudolf's room. One note requested a prior to pray for himself and Mary. Another, to his valet, requested that they be buried in an ordinary grave. A third letter began, 'I must die – that is the only way to leave this world like a gentleman.' And the last words to his wife recognized 'the torment of my presence', and told her to 'be happy in your own way ... I face death calmly – death alone can save my good name.'

Another letter from Rudolf pinpoints the reasons for his suicide: 'The Emperor will not abdicate in the foreseeable future ... Eternal waiting with deeply injurious slights and repeated serious conflicts unbearable ... No understanding anywhere for crushing matrimonial relations.' But his most touching goodbye was to his mistress Mizzi Caspar. According to one of the few people to have seen the note, it was 'overflowing' with love. He had even ensured she would be well looked after by giving her enough money to buy a new house.

### Facing the end

Mary, too, wrote her farewell letters. In one she asked her sister not to 'cry for me, I am crossing over peacefully'. But elsewhere there was a darker message – 'Today he finally confessed to

♔ **Above** *The body of the Crown Prince is removed from Mayerling. He had requested that Mary and he should be buried together in an ordinary grave at Heiligenkreuz, but Rudolf was taken ceremonially to the vault of the Habsburgs while Mary's body was hidden in a linen basket before its hurried and secret burial*

♔ **Below** *Rudolf's faithful valet, Loschek, was the last person to see him alive and the first to see him dead. His memoirs contradict his original statement and Hoyos's account. Did he lie to protect his master?*

Ullstein

A *post mortem* was held on 31 January. The originals of the autopsy findings have disappeared – along with other official papers, possibly including statements by Bratfisch, Loschek, other servants at Mayerling and Mizzi Caspar – but on 2 February an excerpt was published which included the following statements: 'His Imperial and Royal Highness the Crown Prince died from a fracture of the skull and destruction of the front portions of the brain. This fracture was caused by a shot fired against the right anterior temporal area at close range at the right temple. ... The projectile was

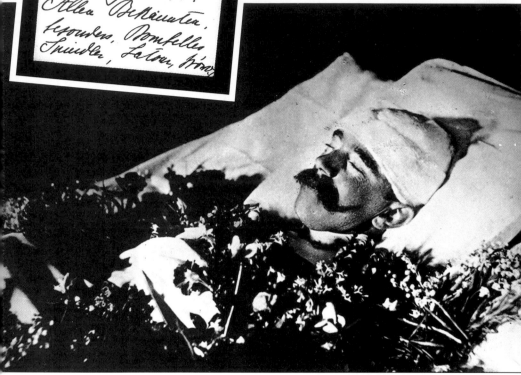

me openly that I could never become his; he has given his father his word of honour that he will break with me. So everything is over.'

### Last rites

The Mayerling affair is riddled with cover-ups which became a necessity from the moment the bodies were found. To discover a Crown Prince dead in his room with a bullet hole through his head is bad enough, but to admit to the presence by his side of a 17-year-old girl with a long history of lovers was too much for the Emperor. So he tried to get out of the mess by pretending she had never been there.

The authorities summoned two of her uncles who dressed up the bloodstained corpse, sat it in the back of a coach propped between them like a life-sized dummy, and drove it at midnight to the cemetery at Heiligenkreuz. Here she was given a hasty burial under police guard and without any religious rites.

Rudolf's funeral was entirely different. After lying in state, with his body decked in flowers, he received a Catholic burial. Technically he should not have had one, but it was argued that he had not been entirely lucid at the time of his death. But if Franz Josef hoped that that was the end of the affair he could not have been more mistaken.

### Anything but the truth

It was the presence of Mary's body beside Rudolf's that was the cause of the cover-up which lead to the myriad versions of the story. At first, it was made known that Rudolf had died alone. Indeed, Helen Vetsera had been obliged to go to Venice to make an announcement, as if her daughter had died there.

At first, it was thought best to conceal the facts out of consideration for Stephanie's position and to prevent the truth about Rudolf's extra-marital liaisons being known. But there was a more sinister reason: getting the sanction for a Catholic burial for Rudolf as a suicide was difficult enough, but as a murderer . . .

Therefore, rumours that he had been murdered were allowed to circulate. As Franz Josef said ten years later, 'Anything is better than the truth.' Some said he had been killed by a blow on the head with a champagne bottle during an orgy; others, that he may have been involved in attempts at a Hungarian rebellion, but lost his nerve at the last minute and was done in by his co-conspirators. It was even thought that Mary had shot Rudolf and that, when his friends discovered the murder, they shot her.

What is more, Franz Josef handed over all papers relating to Mayerling not to the National Archives, but privately to his Prime Minister and lifelong friend, Eduard Taaffe, to keep secret. Taaffe himself did not want the papers published after his death and, to this day, it is not known where they are.

### An enduring legend

In spite of the evidence – sordid as it may seem at times – the fascination with the myth that is Mayerling still endures. For the story of two young lives so full of promise, so tragically and futilely extinguished, will always continue to haunt the annals of royal history.

👑 *The Crown Prince left several farewell letters, but only this one to his wife Stephanie top has been published in full*

👑 *The deathbed above. Rudolf's face was peaceful in death; the bitter smile which had become habitual during the last few months of his life had vanished*

👑 *Mary's lonely grave at Heiligenkreuz right. Her family were not present at her hasty funeral, for that night Count Taaffe had asked Mary's mother, in the Emperor's name, to leave Vienna for a while. She was forbidden to have anything done to her daughter's grave, and put under police surveillance. In the middle of March, the Baroness returned and – still watched by plainclothes detectives – went every week to lay camellias on Mary's grave. The inscription reads 'Man cometh forth like a flower and is cut down'*

MARY
FREIIN V VETSERA